ISLAMIC BELIEF

(Al-ʿAqīdah aṭ-Ṭaḥāwiah)

Imām Abū Jaʿfar aṭ-Ṭaḥāwī
(239–321 A.H.)

UK ISLAMIC ACADEMY

Revised Edition including Arabic Text

ISBN 1 872531 42 3

Published by

UK Islamic Academy,
PO Box 6645,
Leicester,
LE5 5WT.
United Kingdom.

Fax: 00-44-116-221 5905

British Library Cataloguing in Publication Data
A catalogue record for this book is available from the British Library

Printed in England by
Deluxe Printers, 245-a, Acton Lane,
Park Royal, London NW10 7NR

بسم الله الرحمن الرحيم

Preface

Imām Ṭaḥāwī's *al-ʿAqīdah,* representative of the viewpoint of *ahl-as-Sunnah wal-Jamāʿah,* has long been the most widely acclaimed, and indeed indispensable, reference work on Muslim beliefs.

Imām Abū Jaʿfar Aḥmad ibn Muḥammad ibn Salāmah ibn Salmah ibn ʿAbd al-Malik ibn Salmah ibn Sulaim ibn Sulaimān ibn Jawāb Azdi, popularly known as Imām Ṭaḥāwī, after his birthplace in Egypt, is among the most outstanding authorities of the Islāmic world on *Ḥadīth* and *fiqh.* He lived from 239–321 A.H., a time when both the direct and indirect disciples of the four Imāms – Imām Abū Ḥanīfah, Imām Mālik, Imām Shāfiʿī and Imām Aḥmad ibn Ḥanbal – were teaching and practising. This period was the zenith of *Ḥadīth* and *fiqh* studies, and Imām Ṭaḥāwī studied with all the living authorities of the day.

He began as a student of his maternal uncle, Ismaʿīl ibn Yaḥya Muzanī, a leading disciple of Imām Shāfiʿī. Instinctively, however, Imām Ṭaḥāwī felt drawn to the corpus of Imām Abū Ḥanīfah's works. Indeed, he had seen his uncle and teacher turning to the works of Ḥanafī scholars to resolve thorny issues of *fiqh,* drawing heavily on the writings of Imām Muḥammad ibn al-Ḥasan ash-Shaybānī and Imām Abū Yūsuf, who had codified Ḥanafī *fiqh.* This led Imām Ṭaḥāwī to devote his complete attentions to a study of the Ḥanafī works. Eventually he joined the Ḥanafī school.

Imām Ṭaḥāwī stands out not only as a prominent follower of the Ḥanafī school but, in view of his vast erudition and remarkable powers of assimilation, as one of its leading scholars. His monumental scholarly works, such as *Sharḥ Maʿānī al-Āthār* and *Mushkil al-Āthār,* are encyclopaedic in scope and have long been regarded as indispensable for training students in *fiqh.*

Al-ʿAqīdah, though small in size, is a basic text for all times, listing what a Muslim must know and believe in and inwardly comprehend.

There is consensus among the Companions, Successors and all the leading Islāmic authorities such as Imām Abū Ḥanīfah, Imām Abū Yūsuf, Imām Muḥammad, Imām Mālik, Imām Shāfiʿī and Imām Aḥmad ibn Ḥanbal on the doctrines enumerated in this work. For these doctrines shared by *ahl-as-Sunnah wal-Jamāʿah* owe their origin to the Holy Qur'ān and consistent and confirmed *Aḥādīth* – the undisputed primary sources of Islam.

Being a text on Islāmic doctrines, this work draws heavily on arguments set forth in the Holy Qur'ān and the *Sunnah.* Likewise, the arguments advanced in refuting the views of sects that have deviated from the *Sunnah* are also taken from the Holy Qur'ān and the *Sunnah.*

As regards the sects mentioned in this work, a study of Islāmic history up to the time of Imām Ṭaḥāwī would be helpful. References to sects such as *Muʿtazilah, Jahmiyyah, Qadriyyah* and *Jabriyyah* are found in the work. Moreover, it contains allusions to the unorthodox and deviant views of the Shīʿah, Khawārij and such mystics as had departed from the right path. There is an explicit reference in the work to the nonsensical controversy on *khalq-al-Qur'ān* in the times of Ma'mūn and some other ʿAbbāsid Caliphs.

While the permanent relevance of the statements of belief in *al-ʿAqīdah* is obvious, the historical weight and point of certain of these statements can only be properly appreciated if the work is used as a study text under the guidance of some learned person able to elucidate its arguments fully, and with reference to the intellectual and historical background of the sects refuted in the work. Such a study will help one understand Islāmic doctrines better and avoid deviations of the past or present.

Iqbāl Aḥmad Aʿẓami

Leicester, England
Shawwāl 1422 A.H.
January 2002

بسم الله الرحمن الرحيم

In the Name of Allah, the Merciful, the Compassionate

Praise be to Allah, Lord of all the Worlds.

The great scholar Ḥujjat al-Islām Abū Ja'far al-Warrāq aṭ-Ṭaḥāwī al-Misrī, may Allah have mercy on him, said: This is a presentation of the beliefs of *ahl-as-Sunnah wal-Jamā'ah*, according to the school of the jurists of this religion, Abū Ḥanīfah an-Nu'mān ibn Thābit al-Kūfī, Abū Yūsuf Ya'qūb ibn Ibrāhīm al-Anṣārī and Abū 'Abdullāh Muḥammad ibn al-Ḥasan ash-Shaybānī, may Allah be pleased with them all, and what they believe regarding the fundamentals of the religion and their faith in the Lord of all the Worlds.

1. We say about Allah's unity believing – by Allah's help – that Allah is One, without any partners.

2. There is nothing like Him.

3. There is nothing that can overwhelm Him.

4. There is no god other than Him.

5. He is the Eternal without a beginning and enduring without end.

6. He will neither perish nor come to an end.

7. Nothing happens except what He wills.

8. No imagination can conceive of Him and no understanding can comprehend Him.

9. He is different from any created being.

10. He is living and never dies. He is eternally active and never sleeps.

11. He creates without being in need to do so and provides for His creation without effort.

12. He causes death without fear and restores to life without difficulty.

13. He, together with His attributes, has existed since before creation. Bringing creation into existence added nothing to His attributes that was not already there. As He was, together with His attributes, in pre-eternity, so will He remain throughout endless time.

14. It was not only after the act of creation that He could be described as 'the Creator' nor was it only by the act of origination that He could be described as 'the Originator'.

15. He was always the Lord even when there was nothing to be Lord of, and always the Creator even when there was no creation.

16. In the same way that He is the 'Bringer to life of the dead', and deserves this name even before they were brought to life in the first place, so too He deserves the name of 'Creator' before He has created them.

17. This is because He has the power to do everything. Everything is dependent on Him, everything is easy for Him, and He needs for nothing. '*There is nothing like Him and He is the Hearer, the Seer*'. [ash-Shūrā 42: 11]

18. He created creation with His knowledge.

19. He appointed destinies for those He created.

20. He allotted to them fixed life spans.

21. Nothing about them was hidden from Him before He created them, and He knew everything that they would do before He created them.

22. He ordered them to obey Him and forbade them to disobey Him.

23. Everything happens according to His decree and will, and His will is accomplished. The only will that people have is what He wills for them. What He wills for them occurs and what He does not will, does not occur.

24. Out of His generosity, He gives guidance to whoever He wills, protecting and keeping them safe from harm; out of His justice, He leads astray whoever He wills, abasing and afflicting them.

25. All of them are subject to His will whether it be His generosity or His justice.

26. He is exalted beyond having neither opposites nor equals.

27. No one can ward off His decree, put back His command or overpower His affairs.

28. We believe in all of this and are certain that everything comes from Him.

29. We are certain that Muḥammad ﷺ is His chosen servant, selected Prophet and His Messenger with whom He is well pleased.

30. And that he is the seal of the prophets, the Imām of the God-fearing, the most honoured of all the messengers and the beloved of the Lord of all the Worlds.

31. Every claim to prophethood after Him is false and deceitful.

32. He is the one who has been sent to all the *jinn* and all mankind with truth and guidance, with light and illumination.

33. The Qur'ān is the word of Allah. It came from Him as speech without it being possible to say how. He sent it down upon His Messenger as revelation. The believers accept it as absolute truth. They are certain that it is, in truth, the word of Allah.

It was not created like the speech of human beings, and anyone who hears it and claims that it is human speech is an unbeliever. Allah warns him and censures him and threatens him with Fire when He says, Exalted is He: '*I will burn him in the Fire.*' [al-Muddaththir 74: 26] When Allah threatens with Fire those who say '*This is just human speech*' [al-Muddaththir 74: 25] we know for certain that this is rather the speech of the Creator, that it is totally unlike the speech of mankind.

34. Anyone who describes Allah as being in any way the same as a human being is an unbeliever. All those who understand this will take heed and refrain from saying things such as the unbelievers say, and they will know that He, in His attributes, is not like human beings.

35. 'The Seeing of Allah by the People of the Garden' is true, without their vision being all-encompassing and without the manner of their vision being known. As the Book of our Lord has expressed it: '*Faces on that Day radiant, looking at their Lord*'. [al-Qiyāmah 75: 22–3] The explanation of this is as Allah knows and wills. Everything that has come down to us about this from Allah's Messenger ﷺ, in authentic traditions, is as he said and intended. We should not delve into this interpreting it according to our own opinions and letting our imaginations have free rein. No one is safe in his religion unless he surrenders himself completely to Allah, the Exalted and Glorified, and to His Messenger, may Allah bless him and

grant him peace, and unles he leaves the knowledge of things that are ambiguous to the One who knows them.

36. A man's Islām is not secure unless it is based on submission and surrender. Anyone who desires to know things beyond his capacity to know, and whose intellect is not content with surrender, will find that his desire veils him from a pure understanding of Allah's true unity, clear knowledge and correct belief. He will find that he veers between disbelief and belief, confirmation and denial and acceptance and rejection. He will be subject to whisperings and find himself confused and full of doubt, being neither an accepting believer nor a denying rejector.

37. A man's belief in the 'seeing of Allah by the people of the Garden' is incorrect if he tries to imagine what it is like or interprets it according to his own understanding. For the interpretation of this 'seeing', indeed the meaning of any of the subtle phenomena which are in the realm of Lordship, can only be achieved by strict submission. Interpretation must be avoided. Those who do not avoid negating Allah's attributes and of likening Allah to something else, have gone astray and have failed to understand Allah's Glory. For our Lord, the Glorified and the Exalted, can only be described in terms of Oneness and Absolute Singularity. No creation is in any way like Him.

38. He is beyond having limits placed on Him, or being restricted, or having parts or limbs. Nor is He contained by the six directions as all created things are.

39. *Al-Mi'rāj* (the Ascent through the heavens) is true. The Prophet ﷺ, was taken by night and ascended in his bodily form, while awake, through the heavens, to whatever heights Allah willed for him. Allah ennobled him in the way that He ennobled him and revealed to him what He revealed to him,

'*and his heart was not mistaken about what it saw*'. [an-Najm 53: 11] Allah blessed him and granted him peace in this world and the next.

40. *Al-Ḥawḍ,* (the Pool which Allah will grant the Prophet ﷺ as an honour to quench the thirst of His *Ummah* on the Day of Judgement), is true.

41. *Ash-Shafāʿah,* (the intercession, which is stored up for Muslims), is true, as related in the (consistent and confirmed) *Aḥādīth.*

42. The covenant 'which Allah made with Adam and his offspring' is true.

43. Allah knew, before the existence of time, the exact number of those who would enter the Garden and the exact number of those who would enter the Fire. This number will neither be increased nor decreased.

44. The same applies to all actions done by people. They are done exactly as Allah knew they would be done. Everyone is eased to what he was created for and it is the action with which a man's life is sealed which dictates his fate. Those who are fortunate are fortunate by the decree of Allah, and those who are wretched are wretched by the decree of Allah.

45. The exact nature of the decree is Allah's secret in His creation. Neither angel nor Prophet has been given knowledge of it. Delving into this and reflecting too much upon it only leads to destruction and loss, and results in rebelliousness. So be extremely careful about thinking and reflecting on this matter or letting doubts about it assail you. For Allah has kept knowledge of the decree away from human beings, and forbidden them to enquire about it, saying in His Book, '*He is not asked about what He does but they*

are asked. [al-Anbiyā' 21: 23] So anyone who argues: 'Why did Allah do that?' has gone against a judgement of the Book, and anyone who goes against a judgement of the Book is an unbeliever.

46. This, in sum, is what those of Allah's friends with enlightened hearts need to know and what constitutes the degree of those firmly endowed with knowledge. For there are two kinds of knowledge: knowledge which is accessible to created beings, and knowledge which is not accessible to created beings. Denying knowledge which is accessible is disbelief, and claiming knowledge which is inaccessible is also disbelief. Belief can only be firm when accessible knowledge is accepted and inaccessible knowledge is not sought after.

47. We believe in *al-Lawḥ* (the Tablet) and *al-Qalam* (the Pen) and in everything written on it. Even if all created beings were to gather together to make something fail to exist, whose existence Allah had written on the Tablet, they would not be able to do so. And if all created beings were to gather together to make something exist which Allah had not written on it, they would not be able to do so. The Pen has dried having written down all that will be in existence until the Day of Judgement. Whatever a person has missed he would have never got it, and whatever one gets, he would have never missed it.

48. It is necessary for the servant to know that Allah already knows everything that is going to happen in His creation and has decreed it in a detailed and decisive way. There is nothing that He has created in either the heavens or the earth that can contradict it, add to, erase, change, decrease, or increase it in any way. This is a fundamental aspect of belief and a necessary element of all knowledge and recognition of Allah's oneness and Lordship. As Allah says in

His Book: '*He created everything and decreed it in a detailed way*'. [al-Furqān 25: 2] And He also says: '*Allah's command is always a decided decree*'. [al-Aḥzāb 33: 38] So woe to anyone who argues with Allah concerning the decree and who, with a sick heart, begins delving into this matter. In his delusory attempt to investigate the Unseen, he is seeking a secret that can never be uncovered. He ends up an evil-doer, telling nothing but lies.

49. *Al-'Arsh* (the Throne) and *al-Kursī* (the Chair) are true.

50. He is independent of the Throne and what is beneath it.

51. He encompasses everything and is above it, and what He has created is incapable of encompassing Him.

52. We say with belief, acceptance and submission that Allah took Ibrāhīm عليه السلام as an intimate friend and that He spoke directly to Mūsā عليه السلام.

53. We believe in the angels, and the Prophets, and the books which were revealed to the messengers, and we bear witness that they were all following the manifest Truth.

54. We call the people of our *qiblah* Muslims and believers as long as they acknowledge what the Prophet ﷺ, brought, and accept as true everything that he said and told us about.

55. We do not enter into vain talk about Allah nor do we allow any dispute about Allah's religion.

56. We do not argue about the Qur'ān and we bear witness that it is the speech of the Lord of all the Worlds which the Trustworthy Spirit came down with and taught the most honoured of all the Messengers, Muḥammad ﷺ. It is the speech of Allah and no speech of any created being is comparable to it. We do not say that it was created and we

do not go against the consensus of the Muslim community regarding it.

57. We do not consider any of the people of our *qiblah* to be unbelievers because of any wrong action they have done, as long as they do not consider that action to have been lawful.

58. Nor do we say that the wrong action of a man who has belief does not have a harmful effect upon him.

59. We hope that Allah will pardon the people of right action among the believers and grant them entrance into the Garden through His mercy. However, we cannot be certain of this, about any individual and we cannot bear witness that they will definitely be in the Garden (except for the ones named and testified by the messenger of Allah ﷺ that they would be in the Garden). We ask forgiveness for the people of wrong action among the believers and, although we are afraid for them, we are not in despair about them.

60. Both certainty and despair remove one from religion, but the path of truth for the people of the *qiblah* lies between the two (i.e. a person must fear and be conscious of Allah's reckoning as well as be hopeful of Allah's mercy).

61. A person does not step out of belief except by dis–avowing what brought him into it.

62. Belief consists of affirmation by the tongue and acceptance by the heart.

63. And the whole of what is authentically related from the Prophet ﷺ, regarding the *Sharīʿah* and the explanation (of the Qur'ān and of Islām) is true.

64. Belief is, at base, the same for everyone, but the superiority of some over others in it is due to their fear and

awareness of Allah, their opposition to their desires, and their choosing what is more pleasing to Allah.

65. All the believers are 'friends' of Allah and the noblest of them in the sight of Allah are those who are the most obedient and who most closely follow the Qur'ān.

66. Belief consists of belief in Allah, His angels, His books, His messengers, the Last Day, and belief that the Decree – both the good and the evil of it, the sweet and the bitter of it – are all from Allah.

67. We believe in all these things. We do not make any distinction between any of the messengers, we accept as true what each of them brought.

68. Those of the *Ummah* of Muḥammad ﷺ, who have committed grave sins will be in the Fire, but not forever, provided they die and meet Allah as believers affirming His unity – even if they have not repented. They are subject to His will and judgement. If He wants, He will forgive and pardon them out of His generosity. As is mentioned in the Qur'ān when He says: '*And He forgives anything less than that (shirk) to whoever He wills*' [an-Nisā' 4: 116]; and if He wants, He will punish them in the Fire out of His justice and then bring them out of the Fire through His mercy, and for the intercession of those who were obedient to Him, and send them to the Garden. This is because Allah is the Protector of those who recognize Him. He will not treat them in the Next World in the same way as He treats those who deny Him and who are bereft of His guidance and have failed to obtain His protection. O Allah, You are the Protector of Islām and its people; make us firm in Islām until the day we meet You.

69. We agree with performing the prayer behind any of the people of the *qiblah* whether they be right-acting or wrong-

acting, and in performing the funeral prayer over any of them when they die.

70. We do not categorically say that any of them will go to either the Garden or the Fire, and we do not accuse any of them of *kufr* (disbelief), *shirk* (associating partners with Allah), or *nifāq* (hypocrisy), as long as they have not openly demonstrated any of these things. We leave their secrets to Allah.

71. We do not agree with killing any of the *Ummah* of Muḥammad ﷺ, unless it is deemed obligatory to do so by *Sharīʿah.*

72. We do not recognize rebellion against our Imām or those in charge of our affairs even if they are unjust, nor do we wish evil on them, nor do we withdraw from following them. We hold that obedience to them is part of obedience to Allah, The Glorified, and is therefore obligatory as long as they do not order us to commit sins. We pray for right guidance for them and for their wrongs to be pardoned.

73. We follow the *Sunnah* of the Prophet ﷺ and the *Jamāʿah* of the Muslims, and avoid deviation, differences and divisions.

74. We love the people of justice and trustworthiness, and hate the people of injustice and treachery.

75. When our knowledge about something is unclear, we say: 'Allah knows best'.

76. We agree with wiping over leather socks (in *Wuḍū)* whether on a journey or otherwise, just as has come down in the (consistent and confirmed) *aḥādīth.*

77. *Ḥajj* and *jihād* under the leadership of those in charge of the Muslims, whether they are right or wrong-acting, are continuing obligations until the Last Hour comes. Nothing can annul or controvert them.

78. We believe in the *Kirāman Kātibīn,* (the noble angels) who write down our actions. For Allah has appointed the two over us as guardians.

79. We believe in the Angel of Death who is charged with taking the spirits of all the worlds.

80. We believe in the punishment in the grave for those who deserve it, and in the questioning in the grave by the angels *Munkar* and *Nakīr* about one's Lord, one's religion and one's prophet, as has come down in the *aḥādīth* from the Messenger of Allah, may Allah bless him and grant him peace, and what the Companions, may Allah be pleased with them all, have reported.

81. The grave is either one of the meadows of the Garden or one of the pits of the Fire.

82. We believe in being brought back to life after death and in being recompensed for our actions on the Day of Judgement. We also believe in *al-ʿArḍ,* that our actions will be shown and *al-Hisāb,* being brought to account for them. And *Qirā'at al-Kitāb,* reading of the records; in the reward and punishments and in *al-ṣirāṭ* (the Bridge) and *al-Mīzān* (the Balance).

83. The Garden and the Fire having been created never come to an end. We believe that Allah created them before the rest of creation and then created people to inhabit each of them. Out of His bounty, whoever He wills goes to the Garden and out of His justice whoever He wills goes to the Fire. Everybody acts in accordance with what is destined for him and goes towards what he has been created for.

84. Good and evil have both been decreed for people.

85. The capability in terms of *Tawfiq* (Divine Grace and Favour) which makes an action certain to occur cannot be

ascribed to a created being. Such capability is integral with action. Whereas the capability of an action in terms of having the necessary health, ability, being in a position to act and having the necessary means, exists in a person before the action. It is this type of capability which is the object of the dictates of *Sharīʿah.* Allah the Exalted says: '*Allah does not charge a person except according to his ability*'. [al-Baqarah 2: 286]

86. People's actions are created by Allah but earned by people.

87. Allah, the Exalted, has only charged people with what they are able to do and people are only capable of doing what Allah has charged them with (and favoured them to do). This is the explanation of the phrase: 'There is no power and no strength except by Allah.' We add to this that there is no stratagem or way by which anyone can avoid or escape disobedience to Allah except with Allah's help; nor does anyone have the strength to put obedience to Allah into practice and remain firm in it, except if Allah makes it possible for them to do so.

88. Everything happens according to Allah's will, knowledge, predestination and decree. His will overpowers all other wills and His decree overpowers all stratagems. He does whatever He wills and He is never unjust. He is exalted in His purity above all evil and perdition. He is perfect, far beyond any fault or flaw. '*He will not be asked about what He does but they will be asked.*' [al-Anbiyā' 21: 23]

89. There is benefit for dead people in the supplication and alms-giving by the living.

90. Allah responds to people's supplications and gives them what they ask for.

91. Allah has absolute control over everything and nothing has control over Him. Nothing is independent of Allah for the

blinking of an eye. Whoever considers himself independent of Allah even for the blinking of an eye is guilty of unbelief and becomes one of the people of perdition.

92.   Allah is angered and pleased but not in the same way as any creature.

93.   We love the Companions of the Messenger of Allah but we do not take our love for any one individual among them to excess nor do we disown any one of them. We hate anyone who hates them or does not speak well of them and we only speak well of them. Love of them is a part of Islām, part of belief and part of excellent behaviour, while hatred of them is unbelief, hypocrisy and rebelliousness.

94.   We confirm that, after the death of the Messenger of Allah 鑢, the caliphate went first to Abū Bakr aṣ-Ṣiddīq 鑢, thus proving his excellence and superiority over the rest of the Muslims; then to 'Umar ibn al-Khaṭṭāb 鑢; then to 'Uthmān ibn 'Affān 鑢; and then to 'Alī ibn Abī Ṭālib 鑢. These are the Rightly-Guided Caliphs and upright leaders.

95.   We bear witness that the ten who were named by the Messenger of Allah 鑢, and who were promised the Garden by him, will be in the Garden, as the Messenger of Allah 鑢, whose word is truth, bore witness that they would be. The ten are: Abū Bakr, 'Umar, 'Uthmān, 'Alī, Ṭalḥah, Zubayr, Sa'd, Sa'īd, 'Abdur-Raḥmān ibn 'Awf and Abū 'Ubaydah ibn al-Jarrāḥ 鑢 whose title was the trustee of this *Ummah.*

96.   Anyone who speaks well of the Companions of the Messenger of Allah 鑢, and his wives and offspring, who are all pure and untainted by any impurity, is free from the accusation of hypocrisy.

97.   The learned men of the first community and those who followed in their footsteps – the people of virtue, the

narrators of the *Aḥādīth,* the jurists and analysts – must only be spoken about in the best way. Anyone who speaks ill of them is surely not on the right path.

98. We do not prefer any of the saintly men among the *Ummah* over any of the Prophets but rather we say that any one of the Prophets is better than all the *awliyā'* put together.

99. We believe in what we know of *Karāmāt,* the marvels of the *awliyā'* and in authentic stories about them from trustworthy sources.

100. We believe in the signs of the Hour such as the appearance of the Dajjāl and the descent of 'Isā ibn Maryam ﷺ, from heaven. We believe in the rising of the sun from where it sets and in the emergence of the Beast from the earth.

101. We do not accept as true what soothsayers and fortune-tellers say. Nor do we accept the claims of those who affirm anything which goes against the Book, the *Sunnah* and the consensus of the Muslim *Ummah.*

102. We agree that holding together is the true and right path and that separation is deviation and torment.

103. There is only one religion of Allah in the heavens and the earth and that is the religion of Islām. Allah says: '*Surely religion in the sight of Allah is Islam*'. [Āl 'Imrān 3: 19] And He also says: '*I am pleased with Islam as a religion for you*'. [al-Mā'idah 5: 3]

104. Islām lies between going to excess and falling short, between *Tashbīh* (likening of Allah's attributes to anything else), and *Ta'ṭīl* (denying Allah's attributes), between fatalism and refusing decree as proceeding from Allah and between certainty (without being conscious of Allah's reckoning) and despair (of Allah's mercy).

105. This is our religion and it is what we believe in, both inwardly and outwardly, and we renounce any connection, before Allah, with anyone who goes against what we have said and made clear.

We ask Allah to make us firm in our belief and seal our lives with it. To protect us from variant ideas, scattering opinions and evil schools of thought such as those of the *Mushabbihah,* the *Mu'tazilah,* the *Jahmiyyah,* the *Jabriyyah,* the *Qadriyyah* and others like them who go against the *Sunnah* and *Jamā'ah* and have allied themselves with error. We renounce any connection with them and in our opinion they are in error and on the path of destruction.

العقيدة الطحاوية

١

بِسْمِ ٱللَّهِ ٱلرَّحْمَٰنِ ٱلرَّحِيمِ

الحمد لله رب العالمين

قَالَ الْعَلاَّمَةُ حُجَّةُ الإسْلاَمِ أَبُو جَعْفَرٍ الْوَرَّاقُ الطَّحَاوِيُّ - بِمِصْرَ - رَحِمَهُ اللهُ :

هَذَا ذِكْرُ بَيَانِ عَقِيْدَةِ أَهْلِ السُّنَّةِ وَالْجَمَاعَةِ عَلَى مَذْهَبِ فُقَهَاءِ الْمِلَّةِ أَبِيْ حَنِيْفَةَ النُّعْمَانِ بْنِ ثَابِتٍ الْكُوْفِيِّ ، وَأَبِيْ يُوْسُفَ يَعْقُوْبَ بْنِ إبْرَاهِيْمَ الأَنْصَارِيِّ وَأَبِيْ عَبْدِ اللهِ مُحَمَّدِ بْنِ الْحَسَنِ الشَّيْبَانِيِّ رِضْوَانُ اللهِ عَلَيْهِمْ أَجْمَعِيْنَ ، وَما يَعْتَقِدُوْنَ مِن أُصُوْلِ الدِّيْنِ ، وَيَدِيْنُونَ بِهِ لِرَبِّ العَالَمِيْنَ .

١ ـ نَقُوْلُ فِيْ تَوْحِيْدِ اللهِ مُعْتَقِدِيْنَ بِتَوْفِيْقِ اللهِ : إِنَّ اللهَ وَاحِدٌ لاَ شَرِيْكَ لَهُ .

٢ ـ وَلاَ شَيْءَ مِثْلُهُ .

٣ ـ وَلاَ شَيْءَ يُعْجِزُهُ .

٤ ـ وَلَا إِلَهَ غَيْرُهُ.

٥ ـ قَدِيْمٌ بِلَا ابْتِدَاءٍ ، دَائِمٌ بِلَا انْتِهَاءٍ.

٦ ـ لَا يَفْنَى وَلَا يَبِيْدُ.

٧ ـ وَلَا يَكُونُ إِلَّا مَا يُرِيْدُ.

٨ ـ لَا تَبْلُغُهُ الأَوْهَامُ ، وَلَا تُدْرِكُهُ الأَفْهَامُ.

٩ ـ وَلَا يَشْبَهُ الأَنامَ.

١٠ ـ حَيٌّ لَا يَمُوْتُ ، قَيُّومٌ لَا يَنامُ.

١١ ـ خَالِقٌ بِلَا حَاجَةٍ ، رَازِقٌ بِلَا مُؤْنَةٍ.

١٢ ـ مُمِيْتٌ بِلَا مَخافَةٍ ، بَاعِثٌ بِلَا مَشَقَّةٍ.

١٣ ـ مَا زَالَ بِصِفَاتِهِ قَدِيْماً قَبْلَ خَلْقِهِ ، لَمْ يَزْدَدْ بِكَوْنِهِمْ شَيْئاً لَمْ يَكُنْ قَبْلَهُمْ مِنْ صِفَاتِهِ ، وَكَمَا كَانَ بِصِفَاتِهِ أَزَلِيّاً ، كَذَلِكَ لَا يَزَالُ عَلَيْهَا أَبَدِيّاً.

١٤ ـ لَيْسَ بَعْدَ خَلْقِ الْخَلْقِ اسْتَفَادَ اسْمَ «الْخَالِق» ، وَلَا بِإِحْدَاثِ البَرِيَّةِ اسْتَفَادَ اسْمَ «الْبَارِيُ».

١٥ ـ لَهُ مَعْنَى الرُّبُوْبِيَّةِ وَلَا مَرْبُوْب ، وَمَعْنَى الْخَالِقِ وَلَا مَخْلُوْق.

١٦ ـ وَكَمَا أنَّه مُحْيِي الْمَوْتَى بَعْدَما أَحْيَا ، اسْتَحَقَّ هَذَا الاسْمَ قَبْلَ إِحْيَائِهِمْ ، كَذَلِكَ اسْتَحَقَّ اسْمَ الْخَالِقِ قَبْلَ إِنْشَائِهِمْ .

١٧ ـ ذَلِكَ بِأَنَّهُ عَلَى كُلِّ شَيْءٍ قَدِيْرٌ ، وَكُلُّ شَيْءٍ إِلَيْهِ فَقِيْرٌ ، وَكُلُّ أَمْرٍ عَلَيْهِ يَسِيْرٌ ، لَا يَحْتَاجُ إِلَى شَيْءٍ ، ﴿لَيْسَ كَمِثْلِهِۦ شَىْءٌۖ وَهُوَ ٱلسَّمِيعُ ٱلْبَصِيرُ﴾ .

١٨ ـ خَلَقَ الْخَلْقَ بِعِلْمِهِ .

١٩ ـ وَقَدَّرَ لَهُمْ أَقْدَاراً .

٢٠ ـ وَضَرَبَ لَهُمْ آجَالاً .

٢١ ـ وَلَمْ يَخْفَ عَلَيْهِ شَيْءٌ قَبْلَ أَنْ يَخْلُقَهُمْ ، وَعَلِمَ مَا هُمْ عَامِلُوْنَ قَبْلَ أَنْ يَخْلُقَهُمْ .

٢٢ ـ وَأَمَرَهُمْ بِطَاعَتِهِ ، وَنَهَاهُمْ عَنْ مَعْصِيَتِهِ .

٢٣ ـ وَكُلُّ شَيْءٍ يَجْرِيْ بِتَقْدِيْرِهِ وَمَشِيْئَتِهِ ، وَمَشِيْئَتُهُ تُنَفَّذُ وَلَا مَشِيْئَةَ لِلْعِبَادِ إِلَّا مَا شَاءَ لَهُمْ فَمَا شَاءَ لَهُمْ كَانَ ، وَمَا لَمْ يَشَأْ لَمْ يَكُنْ .

٢٤ ـ يَهْدِيْ مَنْ يَشَاءُ ، وَيَعْصِمُ وَيُعَافِيْ ، فَضْلاً ، وَيُضِلُّ مَنْ يَشَاءُ ، وَيَخْذُلُ وَيَبْتَلِيْ ، عَدْلاً .

٢٥ ـ وَكُلُّهُمْ يَتَقَلَّبُوْنَ فِي مَشِيْئَتِهِ ، بَيْنَ فَضْلِهِ وَعَدْلِهِ.

٢٦ ـ وَهُوَ مُتَعَالٍ عَنِ الأَضْدَادِ وَالأَنْدَادِ.

٢٧ ـ لَا رَادَّ لِقَضَائِهِ ، وَلَا مُعَقِّبَ لِحُكْمِهِ ، وَلَا غَالِبَ لأَمْرِهِ.

٢٨ ـ آمَنَّا بِذَلِكَ كُلِّهِ ، وَأَيْقَنَّا أَنَّ كُلًّا مِنْ عِنْدِهِ.

٢٩ ـ وَأَنَّ مُحَمَّداً عَبْدُهُ الْمُصْطَفَى ، وَنَبِيُّهُ الْمُجْتَبَى ، وَرَسُوْلُهُ الْمُرْتَضَى.

٣٠ ـ وَأَنَّهُ خَاتَمُ الأَنْبِيَاءِ ، وَإِمَامُ الأَتْقِيَاءِ ، وَسَيِّدُ الْمُرْسَلِيْنَ وَحَبِيْبُ رَبِّ الْعَالَمِيْنَ.

٣١ ـ وَكُلُّ دَعْوىٰ النُّبُوَّةِ بَعْدَهُ فَغَيٌّ وَهَوىٰ.

٣٢ ـ وَهُوَ الْمَبْعُوْثُ إِلَى عَامَّةِ الْجِنِّ وَكَافَّةِ الْوَرَى ، بِالْحَقِّ وَالْهُدَى ، وَبِالنُّورِ وَالضِّيَاءِ.

٣٣ ـ وَإِنَّ الْقُرْآنَ كَلَامُ اللهِ ، مِنْهُ بَدَا بِلَا كَيفِيَةٍ قَوْلاً وَأَنْزَلَهُ عَلَى رَسُوْلِهِ وَحْياً ، وَصَدَّقَهُ الْمُؤْمِنُوْنَ عَلَى ذَلِكَ حَقّاً ، وَأَيْقَنُوا أَنَّهُ كَلَامُ اللهِ تَعَالَى بِالْحَقِيْقَةِ ، لَيْسَ بِمَخْلُوْقٍ كَكَلَامِ الْبَرِيَّةِ ، فَمَنْ سَمِعَهُ فَزَعَمَ أَنَّهُ كَلَامُ الْبَشَرِ فَقَدْ كَفَرَ ، وَقَدْ ذَمَّهُ اللهُ وَعَابَهُ وَأَوْعَدَهُ بِسَقَرَ ، حَيْثُ قَالَ تَعَالَى: ﴿ سَأُصْلِيهِ

سَقَرَ ﴿٢٦﴾﴾ [المدثر: ٢٦] فَلَمَّا أَوْعَدَ اللهُ بِسَقَرَ لِمَنْ قَالَ: ﴿إِنْ هَٰذَآ إِلَّا قَوْلُ ٱلْبَشَرِ﴾ [المدثر: ٢٥]، عَلِمْنَا وَأَيْقَنَّا أَنَّهُ قَوْلُ خَالِقِ الْبَشَرِ، وَلَا يُشْبِهُ قَولَ الْبَشَرِ.

٣٤ ـ وَمَنْ وَصَفَ اللهَ بِمَعْنًى مِن مَعَانِي الْبَشَرِ، فَقَدْ كَفَرَ، «فَ» (١) مَنْ أَبْصَرَ هَذَا اعْتَبَرَ، وَعَنْ مِثْلِ قَوْلِ الْكُفَّارِ انْزَجَرَ، «وَ» (٢) عَلِمَ أَنَّهُ بِصِفَاتِهِ لَيْسَ كَالْبَشَرِ.

٣٥ ـ وَالرُّؤْيَةُ حَقٌّ لأَهْلِ الْجَنَّةِ، بِغَيْرِ إِحَاطَةٍ وَلَا كَيْفِيَّةٍ، كَمَا نَطَقَ بِهِ كِتَابُ رَبِّنَا: ﴿وُجُوهٌ يَوْمَئِذٍ نَّاضِرَةٌ ﴿٢٢﴾ إِلَىٰ رَبِّهَا نَاظِرَةٌ﴾ [القيامة: ٢٢ ـ ٢٣]. وَتَفْسِيرُهُ عَلَى مَا أَرَادَهُ اللهُ تَعَالَى وَعَلِمَهُ، وَكُلُّ مَا جَاءَ فِيْ ذَلِكَ فِي الْحَدِيْثِ الصَّحِيْحِ عَنْ رَسُوْلِ اللهِ ﷺ فَهُوَ كَمَا قَالَ، وَمَعْنَاهُ عَلَى مَا أَرَادَ، لَا نَدْخُلُ فِي ذَلِكَ مُتَأَوِّلِيْنَ بِآرَائِنَا، وَلَا مُتَوَهِّمِيْنَ بِأَهْوَائِنَا، فَإِنَّهُ مَا سَلِمَ فِي دِيْنِهِ إِلَّا مَنْ سَلَّمَ للهِ عَزَّ وَجَلَّ وَلِرَسُولِهِ ﷺ، وَرَدَّ عِلْمَ مَا اشْتَبَهَ عَلَيْهِ إِلَى عَالِمِه.

٣٦ ـ وَلَا تَثْبُتُ قَدَمُ الإِسْلَامِ إِلَّا عَلَى ظَهْرِ التَّسْلِيْمِ وَالإِسْتِسْلَامِ، فَمَن رَامَ عِلْمَ مَا حُظِرَ عَنْهُ عِلْمُهُ، وَلَمْ يَقْنَعْ بِالتَّسْلِيْمِ فَهْمُهُ، حَجَبَهُ مَرَامُهُ عَنْ خَالِصِ التَّوْحِيْدِ، وَصَافِي الْمَعْرِفَةِ، وَصَحِيْحِ الإِيْمَانِ، فَيَتَذَبْذَبُ بَيْنَ الْكُفْرِ وَالإِيْمَانِ،

وَالتَّصْدِيْقِ والتَّـكْذِيْبِ ، وَالإِقْرَارِ وَالإِنْكَارِ ، مُوَسْوَساً تَائِهاً ، شَاكّاً ، لاَ مُؤْمِناً مُصَدِّقاً ، وَلاَ جَاحِداً مُـكَذِّباً .

٣٧ ـ وَلاَ يَصِحُّ الإِيْمَانُ بالرُّؤْيَةِ لأَهْلِ دَارِ السَّلاَمِ لِمَنِ اعْتَبَرَهَا مِنْهُمْ بِوَهْمٍ ، أَوْ تَأَوَّلَهَا بِفَهْمٍ إِذْ كَان تَأْوِيْلُ الرُّؤْيَةِ ـ وَتَأْوِيْلُ كُلِّ مَعْنًى يُضَافُ إِلَى الرُّبُوْبِيَّةِ ـ بِتَرْكِ التَّأْوِيْلِ وَلُزُوْمِ التَّسْلِيْـمِ ، وَعَلَيْـهِ دِيْـنُ الْمُسْلِمِيْـنَ . وَمَـنْ لَـمْ يَتَـوَقَّ النَّفْيَ وَالتَّشْبِيْه ، زَلَّ وَلَمْ يُصِبِ التَّـنْزِيْهَ ، فَإِنَّ رَبَّنَا جَلَّ وَعَلاَ مَوْصُوْفٌ بِصِفَاتِ الوَحْدَانِيَّةِ ، مَنْعُوْتٌ بِنُعُوْتِ الْفَرْدَانِيَّةِ ، لَيْسَ فِي مَعْنَاهُ أَحَدٌ مِنَ الْبَرِيَّةِ .

٣٨ ـ وَتَعَالَى عَنْ الحُدُوْدِ وَالْغَايَاتِ ، وَالأَرْكَانِ وَالأَعْضَاءِ وَالأَدَوَاتِ ، لاَ تَحْوِيْهِ الْجِهَاتُ السِّتُّ كَسَائِرِ الْمُبْتَدَعَاتِ .

٣٩ ـ وَالْمِعْـرَاجُ حَـقٌّ وَقَـدْ أُسْرِيَ بِالنَّبِـيِّ ﷺ ، وَعُـرِجَ بِشَخْصِهِ فِي الْيَقَظَةِ إِلَى السَّمَاءِ ، ثُمَّ إِلَى حَيْثُ شَاءَ اللهُ مِنَ الْعُلاَ ، وَأَكْرَمَهُ اللهُ بِمَا شَاءَ ، وَأَوْحَى إِلَيْهِ مَا أَوْحَى ، ﴿مَا كَذَبَ ٱلْفُؤَادُ مَا رَأَىٰٓ ﴿١١﴾﴾ فَصَلَّى اللهُ عَلَيْهِ وَسَلَّمَ فِي الآخِرَةِ وَالأُوْلَى .

٤٠ ـ وَالْحَوْضُ الَّذي أَكْرَمَهُ اللهُ تَعالَى بِهِ ـ غِيَاثاً لأُمَّتِهِ ـ حَقٌّ .

٤١ ـ والشَّفَاعَةُ الَّتِي ادَّخَرَهَا لَهُمْ حَقٌّ ، كَمَا رُوِيَ فِي الأَخْبَارِ.

٤٢ ـ وَالْمِيْثَاقُ الَّذِي أَخَذَهُ اللهُ تَعَالَى مِنْ آدَمَ وَذُرِّيَّتِهِ حَقٌّ.

٤٣ ـ وَقَدْ عَلِمَ اللهُ تَعَالَى فِيْمَا لَمْ يَزَلْ عَدَدَ مَنْ يَدْخُلُ الْجَنَّةَ ، وَعَدَدَ مَنْ يَدْخُلُ النَّارَ ، جُمْلَةً وَاحِدَةً ، فَلاَ يَزْدَادُ فِي ذَلِكَ الْعَدَدِ ، وَلاَ يَنْقُصُ مِنْهُ.

٤٤ ـ وَكَذَلِكَ أَفْعَالُهُمْ فِيمَا عَلِمَ مِنْهُمْ أَنْ يَفْعَلُوْهُ وَكُلٌّ مُيَسَّرٌ لِمَا خُلِقَ لَهُ ، وَالأَعْمَالُ بِالْخَوَاتِيْمِ ، وَالسَّعِيْدُ مَنْ سَعِدَ بِقَضَاءِ اللهِ ، وَالشَّقِيُّ مَنْ شَقِيَ بِقَضَاءِ اللهِ.

٤٥ ـ وَأَصْلُ الْقَدَرِ سِرُّ اللهِ تَعَالَى فِيْ خَلْقِهِ ، لَمْ يَطَّلِعْ عَلَى ذَلِكَ مَلَكٌ مُقَرَّبٌ وَلاَ نَبِيٌّ مُرْسَلٌ وَالتَّعَمُّقُ وَالنَّظَرُ فِي ذَلِكَ ذَرِيْعَةُ الْخُذْلاَنِ ، وَسُلَّمُ الْحِرْمَانِ ، وَدَرَجَةُ الطُّغْيَانِ ، فَالْحَذَرَ كُلَّ الْحَذَرِ مِن ذَلِكَ نَظَراً أَوْ فِكْراً أَوْ وَسْوَسَةً ، فَإِنَّ اللهَ تَعَالَى طَوَى عِلْمَ الْقَدَرِ عَنْ أَنَامِهِ ، وَنَهَاهُمْ عَنْ مَرَامِهِ ، كَمَا قَالَ تَعَالَى فِي كِتَابِهِ: ﴿لَا يُسْـَٔلُ عَمَّا يَفْعَلُ وَهُمْ يُسْـَٔلُونَ﴾ [الأنبياء: ٢٣] ، فَمَنْ سَأَلَ: لِمَ فَعَل؟ فَقَدْ رَدَّ حُكْمَ الْكِتَابِ ، وَمَنْ رَدَّ حُكْمَ الْكِتَابِ كَانَ مِنَ الْكَافِرِيْنَ.

٤٦ ـ فَهَذَا جُمْلَةُ مَا يَحْتَاجُ إِلَيْهِ مَنْ هُوَ مُنَوَّرٌ قَلْبُهُ مِنْ أَوْلِيَاءِ اللهِ تَعَالَى ، وَهِيَ دَرَجَةُ الرَّاسِخِيْنَ فِي الْعِلْم ، لأَنَّ الْعِلْمَ عِلْمَانِ: عِلْمٌ في الْخَلْقِ مَوْجُوْدٌ ، وَعِلْمٌ فِي الْخَلْقِ مَفْقُوْدٌ ، فَإِنْكَارُ الْعِلْمِ الْمَوْجُوْدِ كُفْرٌ ، وَادِّعَاءُ الْعِلْمِ الْمَفْقُوْدِ كُفْرٌ ، وَلاَ يَثْبُتُ الإِيْمَانُ إِلاَ بِقَبُوْلِ الْعِلْمِ الْمَوْجُوْدِ وَتَرْكِ طَلَبِ الْعِلْمِ الْمَفْقُوْدِ.

٤٧ ـ وَنُؤْمِنُ بِاللَّوْحِ وَالْقَلَمِ وَبِجَمِيْعِ مَا فِيْهِ قَدْ رُقِمَ ، فَلَو اجْتَمَعَ الْخَلْقُ كُلُّهُمْ عَلَى شَيْءٍ كَتَبَهُ اللهُ تَعَالَى فِيْهِ أَنَّهُ كَائِنٌ ، لِيَجْعَلُوْهُ غَيْرَ كَائِنٍ لَمْ يَقْدِرُوْا عَلَيْهِ وَلو اجْتَمَعُوا كُلُّهُمْ عَلى شَيْءٍ لَمْ يَكْتُبْهُ اللهُ تَعَالَى فِيْهِ ، لِيَجْعَلُوْهُ كَائِناً ـ لَمْ يَقْدِرُوْا عَلَيْهِ ـ جَفَّ الْقَلَمُ بمَا هُوَ كَائِنٌ إِلَى يَوْم الْقِيَامَةِ ، وَما أَخْطَأَ الْعَبْدَ لَمْ يَكُنْ لِيُصِيْبَهُ ، وَمَا أَصَابَهُ لَمْ يَكُنْ لِيُخْطِأَهُ.

٤٨ ـ وَعَلى الْعَبْدِ أَنْ يَعْلَمَ أَنَّ اللهَ قَدْ سَبَقَ عِلْمُهُ فِي كُلِّ كَائِنٍ مِنْ خَلْقِهِ ، فَقَدَّرَ ذَلِكَ تَقْدِيْراً مُحْكَماً مُبْرَماً ، لَيْسَ فِيْهِ نَاقِضٌ ، وَلاَ مُعَقِّبٌ ، وَلاَ مُزِيلٌ وَلاَ مُغَيِّرٌ ، وَلاَ نَاقِصٌ وَلاَ زَائِدٌ مِنْ خَلْقِهِ فِي سَمَاوَاتِهِ وَأَرْضِهِ ، وَذَلِكَ مِنَ عَقَدِ الإِيْمَانِ ، وَأُصُوْلِ الْمَعْرِفَةِ ، والاعْتِرَافُ بِتَوْحِيْدِ اللهِ تَعَالَى وَرُبُوْبِيَّتِهِ ، كَمَا قَالَ تَعَالَى فِي كِتابهِ العزيز: ﴿ وَخَلَقَ كُلَّ شَيْءٍ

﴿فَقَدَّرَهُۥ تَقۡدِيرٗا﴾ [الفرقان: ٢]، وَقَالَ تَعَالَى: ﴿وَكَانَ أَمۡرُ ٱللَّهِ قَدَرٗا مَّقۡدُورًا﴾ [الأحزاب: ٣٨].

فَوَيْلٌ لِمَنْ صَارَ للهِ تَعَالَى فِي الْقَدَرِ خَصِيْماً، وَأَحْضَرَ لِلنَّظَرِ فِيْهِ قَلْباً سَقِيْماً، لَقَدْ الْتَمَسَ بِوَهْمِهِ فِي فَحْصِ الْغَيْبِ سِرّاً كَتِيْماً، وَعَادَ بِمَا قَالَ فِيْهِ أَفَّاكاً أَثِيْماً.

٤٩ ـ وَالعَرْشُ وَالْكُرْسِيُّ حَقٌّ.

٥٠ ـ وَهُوَ مُسْتَغْنٍ عَنِ الْعَرْشِ وَمَا دُوْنَهُ.

٥١ ـ مُحِيطٌ بِكُلِّ شَيْءٍ وَبِمَا فَوْقَهُ، وَقَد أَعْجَزَ عَنِ الإِحَاطَةِ خَلْقَهُ.

٥٢ ـ وَنَقُوْلُ: إِنَّ اللهَ اتَّخَذَ إِبْرَاهِيْمَ خَلِيْلاً، وَكَلَّمَ مُوْسَى تَكْلِيْماً، إِيْمَاناً وَتَصْدِيْقاً، وَتَسْلِيْماً.

٥٣ ـ وَنُؤْمِنُ بِالْمَلائِكَةِ وَالنَّبِيِّيْنَ، وَالْكُتُبِ الْمُنَزَّلَةِ عَلَى الْمُرْسَلِيْنَ وَنَشْهَدُ أَنَّهُمْ كَانُوْا عَلَى الْحَقِّ الْمُبِيْنِ.

٥٤ ـ وَنُسَمِّيْ أَهْلَ قِبْلَتِنَا مُسْلِمِيْنَ مُؤْمِنِيْنَ، مَا دَامُوْا بِمَا جَاءَ بِهِ النَّبِيُّ ﷺ مُعْتَرِفِيْنَ، وَلَهُ بِكُلِّ مَا قَالَهُ وَأَخْبَرَ مُصَدِّقِيْنَ.

٥٥ ـ وَلاَ نَخُوْضُ فِي اللهِ، وَلاَ نُمَارِيْ فِيْ دِيْنِ اللهِ.

٥٦ ـ وَلاَ نُجَادِلُ فِي الْقُرْآنِ، وَنَشْهَدُ أَنَّهُ كَلاَمُ رَبِّ

الْعَالَمِيْنَ ، نَزَلَ بِهِ الرُّوْحُ الأَمِيْنُ ، فَعَلَّمَهُ سَيِّدَ الْمُرْسَلِيْنَ محمداً ﷺ ، وَهُوَ كَلامُ اللهِ تَعَالَى ، لاَ يُسَاوِيْهِ شَيْءٌ مِنْ كَلاَمِ الْمَخْلُوْقِيْنَ ، وَلاَ نَقُوْلُ بِخَلْقِهِ ، وَلاَ نُخَالِفُ جَمَاعَةَ الْمُسْلِمِيْنَ .

٥٧ ـ وَلاَ نُكَفِّرُ أَحَداً مِنْ أَهْلِ الْقِبْلَةِ بِذَنْبٍ ، مَالَمْ يَسْتَحِلَّهُ .

٥٨ ـ وَلاَ نَقُولُ لاَ يَضُرُّ مَعَ الإِيْمَانِ ذَنْبٌ لِمَنْ عَمِلَهُ .

٥٩ ـ وَنَرْجُوْ لِلْمُحْسِنِيْنَ مِن الْمُؤْمِنِيْنَ أَنْ يَعْفُوَ عَنْهُمْ وَيُدْخِلَهُمُ الْجَنَّةَ بِرَحْمَتِهِ وَلاَ نَأْمَنُ عَلَيْهِمْ ، وَلاَ نَشْهَدُ لَهُمْ بِالْجَنَّةِ ، وَنَسْتَغْفِرُ لِمُسِيْئِهِمْ وَنَخَافُ عَلَيْهِمْ ، وَلاَ نُقَنِّطُهُمْ .

٦٠ ـ والأَمْنُ وَالإِيَاسُ يَنْقُلاَنِ عَنْ مِلَّةِ الإِسْلاَمِ ، وَسَبِيلُ الْحَقِّ بَيْنَهُمَا لأَهْلِ الْقِبْلَةِ .

٦١ ـ وَلاَ يَخْرُجُ الْعَبْدُ مِنَ الإِيْمَانِ إِلاَّ بِجُحُوْدِ مَا أَدْخَلَهُ فِيْهِ .

٦٢ ـ والإِيْمَانُ: هُوَ الإِقْرَارُ بِاللِّسَانِ ، والتَّصْدِيْقُ بِالْجَنَانِ .

٦٣ ـ وَجَمِيْعُ مَا صَحَّ عَنْ رَسُولِ اللهِ ﷺ مِنَ الشَّرْعِ وَالْبَيَانِ كُلُّهُ حَقٌّ.

٦٤ ـ وَالإِيْمَانُ وَاحِدٌ، وَأَهْلُهُ فِي أَصْلِهِ سَوَاءٌ والتَّفَاضُلُ بَيْنَهُمْ بالْخَشيَّةِ والتُّـقَى، وَمُخَالَفَةِ الْهَوَى، وَمُلازَمَةِ الأَوْلَى.

٦٥ ـ وَالْمُؤْمِنُوْنَ كُلُّهُمْ أَوْلِيَاءُ الرَّحْمَنِ، وَأَكْرَمُهُمْ عِنْدَ اللهِ أَطْوَعُهُمْ وَأَتْبَعُهُمْ لِلْقُرْآنِ.

٦٦ ـ وَالإِيْمَانُ: هُوَ الإِيْمَانُ باللهِ، وَمَلاَئِكَتِهِ، وَكُتُبِهِ، وَرُسُلِهِ، وَالْيَوم الآخِرِ، وَالْقَدَرِ، خَيْرِهِ وشَرِّهِ، وَحُلْوِهِ وَمُرِّهِ، مِنَ اللهِ تَعَالَىٰ.

٦٧ ـ وَنَحْنُ مُؤْمِنُوْنَ بِذَلِكَ كُلِّهِ، ولاَ نُفَرِّقُ بَيْنَ أَحَدٍ مِنْ رُسُلِهِ، وَنُصَدِّقُهُمْ كُلَّهُمْ عَلَى مَا جَاؤُوْا بِهِ.

٦٨ ـ وَأَهْـلُ الْكَبَـائِـرِ مِـنْ أُمَّـةِ مُحَمَّـدٍ ﷺ فِـي النَّـارِ لا يَخْلُدُوْنَ، إِذَا مَاتُـوْا وَهُـمْ مُوَحِّـدُوْنَ، وَإِنْ لَمْ يَـكُوْنُـوا تائِبِيْنَ بَعْدَ أَنْ لَقُوا اللهَ عَارِفِيْنَ مُؤْمِنِيْنَ وَهُمْ فِي مَشِيْئَتِهِ وَحُكْمِهِ، إِن شَاءَ غَفَرَ لَهُمْ وَعَفَا عَنْهُمْ بِفَضْلِهِ، كَمَا ذَكَرَ عَزَّ وَجَلَّ فِي كِتَابِهِ: ﴿ إِنَّ ٱللَّهَ لَا يَغْفِرُ أَن يُشْرَكَ بِهِۦ وَيَغْفِرُ مَا دُونَ ذَٰلِكَ لِمَن يَشَآءُ ﴾ [النساء: ٤٨ و١١٦] وَإِنْ شَاءَ عَذَّبَهُمْ فِي النَّارِ بِعَدْلِهِ،

ثُمَّ يُخْرِجُهُمْ مِنْهَا بِرَحْمَتِهِ وَشَفَاعَةِ الشَّافِعِيْنَ مِنْ أَهلِ طَاعَتِهِ ، ثُمَّ يَبْعَثُهُمْ إلى جَنَّتِهِ ، وَذَلِكَ بِأَنَّ اللهَ تَعَالَى تَوَلَّى أَهْلَ مَعْرِفَتِهِ ، وَلَمْ يَجْعَلْهُمْ في الدَّارَيْنِ كَأَهْلِ نُكْرَتِهِ ، الَّذِيْنَ خَابُوْا مِنْ هِدَايَتِهِ ، وَلَمْ يَنَالُوْا مِنْ وَلَايَتِهِ ، اللَّهُمَّ يَا وَلِيَّ الإِسْلَامِ وَأَهْلِهِ ، ثَبِّتْنَا عَلَى الإِسْلامِ حَتَّى نَلْقَاكَ بِهِ.

٦٩ ـ ونَرَى الصَّلاةَ خَلْفَ كُلِّ بَرٍّ وَفَاجِرٍ مِنْ أَهْلِ الْقِبْلَةِ وعَلَى مَنْ مَاتَ مِنْهُمْ.

٧٠ ـ وَلَا نُنَزِّلُ أَحَداً مِنْهُمْ جَنَّةً وَلَا نَاراً ، وَلَا نَشْهَدُ عَلَيْهِمْ بِكُفْرٍ وَلَا بِشِرْكٍ وَلَا بِنِفَاقٍ ، مَالَمْ يَظْهَرْ مِنْهُمْ شَيْءٌ مِنْ ذَلِكَ ، وَنَذَرُ سَرَائِرَهُمْ إِلَى اللهِ تَعَالَى.

٧١ ـ وَلَا نَرَى السَّيْفَ عَلَى أَحَدٍ مِنْ أُمَّةِ مُحَمَّدٍ ﷺ إِلَّا مَنْ وَجَبَ عَلَيْهِ السَّيْفُ.

٧٢ ـ وَلَا نَرَى الْخُرُوْجَ عَلَى أَئِمَّتِنَا وَوُلَاةِ أُمُوْرِنَا ، وَإِنْ جَارُوْا ، وَلَا نَدْعُوْ عَلَيْهِمْ ، وَلَا نَنْزِعُ يَداً مِنْ طَاعَتِهِمْ ، ونَرَى طَاعَتَهُمْ مِنْ طَاعَةِ اللهِ عَزَّ وَجَلَّ فَرِيْضَةً ، مَالَمْ يَأْمُرُوْا بِمَعْصِيَةٍ ، وَنَدْعُوْ لَهُمْ بالصَّلَاحِ وَالْمُعَافَاةِ.

٧٣ ـ وَنَتَّبِعُ السُّنَّةَ وَالْجَمَاعَةَ ، وَتَجْتَنِبُ الشُّذُوْذَ وَالْخِلَافَ وَالْفُرْقَةَ.

٧٤ ـ وَنُحِبُّ أَهْلَ الْعَدْلِ وَالأَمَانَةِ ، وَنَبْغَضُ أَهْلَ الْجَوْرِ وَالْخِيَانَةِ .

٧٥ ـ وَنَقُوْلُ : اللهُ أَعْلَمُ ، فِيْمَا اشْتَبَهَ عَلَيْنَا عِلْمُهُ .

٧٦ ـ وَنَـرَى الْمَسْحَ عَلَى الْخُفَّيْنِ فِي السَّفَرِ وَالْحَضَرِ كَمَا جَاءَ فِي الأَثَـرِ .

٧٧ ـ وَالْحَـجُّ وَالْجِهَـادُ مَـاضِيَـانِ مَـعَ أُولِـى الأَمْـرِ مِـنَ الْمُسْلِمِيْنَ بَرِّهِمْ وَفَاجِرِهِمْ إِلَى قِيَامِ السَّاعَةِ ، لاَ يُبْطِلُهُمَا شَيْءٌ وَلاَ يَنْقُضُهُمَا .

٧٨ ـ وَنُؤْمِنُ بالْكِرَامِ الكَاتِـبِيْنَ ، فَإِنَّ اللهَ قَدْ جَعَلَهُمْ عَلَيْنَا حَافِظِيْنَ .

٧٩ ـ وَنُؤْمِنُ بِمَلَكِ الْمَوتِ ، الْمُوَكَّلِ بِقَبْضِ أَرْوَاحِ الْعَالَمِيْنَ .

٨٠ ـ وَبِعَذَابِ الْقَبْرِ لِمَنْ كَانَ لَهُ أَهْلاً ، وَسُؤَالِ مُنْكَرٍ وَنَكِيْرٍ فِي قَبْرِهِ عَنْ رَبِّه وَدِيْنِهِ وَنَبِيِّهِ ، عَلَىَ مَا جَاءَتْ بِهِ الأَخْبَارُ عَنْ رَسُولِ اللهِ ﷺ ، وَعَنِ الصَّحَابَةِ رِضْوَانُ اللهِ عَلَيْهِمْ .

٨١ ـ وَالْقَبْـرُ رَوْضَـةٌ مِنْ رِيَـاضِ الْجَنَّـةِ ، أَوْ حُفْـرَةٌ مِنْ حُفَـرِ النِّيرَانِ .

٨٢ ـ وَنُؤْمِنُ بِالْبَعْثِ وَجَزَاءِ الأَعْمَالِ يَوْمَ الْقِيَامَةِ ، وَالْعَرْضِ وَالْحِسَابِ ، وَقِرَاءَةِ الْكِتَابِ ، وَالثَّوَابِ وَالْعِقَابِ ، وَالصِّرَاطِ وَالْمِيْزَانِ .

٨٣ ـ وَالْجَنَّةُ وَالنَّارُ مَخْلُوْقَتَانِ لاَ تَفْنَيَانِ أَبداً وَلاَ تَبِيْدَانِ ، وَأَنَّ اللهَ تَعَالَى خَلَقَ الْجَنَّةَ وَالنَّارَ قَبْلَ الْخَلْقِ ، وَخَلَقَ لَهُمَا أَهْلاً ، فَمَنْ شَاءَ مِنْهُمْ إِلَى الْجَنَّةِ فَضْلاً مِنْهُ ، وَمَنْ شَاءَ مِنْهُمْ إِلَى النَّارِ عَدْلاً مِنْهُ ، وَكُلٌّ يَعْمَلُ لِمَا قَدْ فُرِغَ لَهُ ، وَصَائِرٌ إِلَى مَا خُلِقَ لَهُ .

٨٤ ـ وَالْخَيْرُ وَالشَّرُّ مُقَدَّرَانَ عَلَى الْعِبَادِ .

٨٥ ـ وَالاِسْتِطَاعَةُ الَّتِيْ يَجِبُ بِهَا الْفِعْلُ ، مِنْ نَحْوِ التَّوْفِيقِ الَّذِي لاَ يَجُوْزُ أَنْ يُوْصَفَ الْمَخْلُوْقُ بِهِ ـ فَهِيَ مَعَ الْفِعْلِ ، وَأَمَّا الإِسْتِطَاعَةُ مِنْ جِهَةِ الصِّحَّةِ وَالْوُسْعِ ، وَالتَّمَكُّنِ وَسَلاَمَةِ الآلاَتِ ـ فَهِيَ قَبْلَ الْفِعْلِ ، وَبِهَا يَتَعَلَّقُ الْخِطَابُ ، وَهُوَ كَمَا قَالَ تَعَالَى : ﴿لَا يُكَلِّفُ ٱللَّهُ نَفْسًا إِلَّا وُسْعَهَا﴾ [البقرة : ٢٨٦] .

٨٦ ـ وَأَفْعَالُ الْعِبَادِ خَلْقُ اللهِ ، وَكَسْبٌ مِنَ الْعِبَادِ .

٨٧ ـ وَلَمْ يُكَلِّفْهُمُ اللهُ تَعَالَى إِلاَّ مَا يُطِيْقُوْنَ ، وَلاَ يُطِيْقُوْنَ إِلاَّ مَا كَلَّفَهُمْ وَهُوَ تَفْسِيرُ : «لاَ حَوْلَ وَلاَ قُوَّةَ إِلاَّ بِاللهِ» ، نَقُوْلُ :

لَا حِيْلَةَ لأَحَدٍ ، وَلَا حَرَكَةَ لأَحَدٍ وَلَا تَحَوُّلَ لأَحَدٍ عَنْ مَعْصِيَةِ اللهِ إِلَّا بِمُعُوْنَةِ اللهِ ، وَلَا قُوَّةَ لأَحَدٍ عَلَى إِقَامَةِ طَاعَةِ اللهِ وَالثَّبَاتِ عَلَيْهَا إِلَّا بِتَوْفِيْقِ اللهِ .

٨٨ ـ وَكُلُّ شَيْءٍ يَجْرِي بِمَشِيْئَةِ اللهِ تَعَالَى وَعِلْمِهِ وَقَضَائِهِ وَقَدَرِهِ غَلَبَتْ مَشِيْئَتُهُ الْمَشِيْئَاتِ كُلَّهَا ، وَغَلَبَ قَضَاؤُهُ الْحِيَلَ كُلَّهَا يَفْعَلُ مَا يَشَاءُ ، وَهُوَ غَيْرُ ظَالِمٍ أَبَداً تَقَدَّسَ عَنْ كُلِّ سُوْءٍ وَحَيْنٍ ، وَتَنَزَّهَ عَنْ كُلِّ عَيْبٍ وَشَيْنٍ ، ﴿لَا يُسْئَلُ عَمَّا يَفْعَلُ وَهُمْ يُسْئَلُونَ﴾ [الأنبياء : ٢٣].

٨٩ ـ وَفِي دُعَاءِ الأَحْيَاءِ وَصَدَقَاتِهِمْ مَنْفَعَةٌ لِلأَمْوَاتِ .

٩٠ ـ وَاللهُ تَعَالَى يَسْتَجِيْبُ الدَّعْوَاتِ ، وَيَقْضِي الْحَاجَاتِ .

٩١ ـ وَيَمْلِكُ كُلَّ شَيْءٍ ، وَلَا يَمْلِكُهُ شَيْءٌ وَلَا غِنىً عَنِ اللهِ تَعَالَى طَرْفَةَ عَيْنٍ ، وَمَنِ اسْتَغْنَى عَنِ اللهِ طَرْفَةَ عَيْنٍ فَقَدْ كَفَرَ وَصَارَ مِنْ أَهْلِ الْحَيْنِ .

٩٢ ـ واللهُ يَغْضَبُ وَيَرْضَى ، لَا كَأَحَدٍ مِنَ الْوَرَى .

٩٣ ـ وَنُحِبُّ أَصْحَابَ رَسُوْلِ اللهِ ﷺ ، وَلَا نُفْرِطُ فِي حُبِّ أَحَدٍ مِنْهُمْ وَلَا نَتَبَرَّأُ مِنْ أَحَدٍ مِنْهُمْ ، وَنُبْغِضُ مَنْ يُبْغِضُهُمْ ، وَبِغَيْرِ الْخَيْرِ يَذْكُرُهُمْ ، وَلَا نَذْكُرُهُمْ إِلَّا بِخَيْرٍ ، وَحُبُّهُمْ دِيْنٌ

وَإِيْمَانٌ وَإِحْسَانٌ ، وَبُغْضُهُمْ كُفْرٌ وَنِفَاقٌ وَطُغْيَانٌ .

٩٤ ـ وَنُثْبِتُ الْخِلاَفَةَ بَعْدَ رَسُول اللهِ ﷺ أَوَّلاً لأَبِي بَكْرٍ الصِّدِّيْقِ رَضِيَ اللهُ عَنْهُ ، تَفْضِيْلاً لَهُ وَتَقْدِيْماً عَلى جَمِيْعِ الأُمَّةِ ، ثُمَّ لِعُمَرَ بْنِ الْخَطَّابِ رَضِيَ اللهُ عَنْهُ ، ثُمَّ لِعُثْمَانَ رَضِيَ اللهُ عَنْهُ ، ثُمَّ لِعَلِيٍّ بْنِ أَبِي طَالِبٍ رَضِيَ اللهُ عَنْهُ ، وَهُمْ الْخُلَفَاءُ الرَّاشِدُوْنَ والأَئِمَّةُ الْمُهْتَدُوْنَ .

٩٥ ـ وأَنَّ الْعَشَرَةَ الَّذِيْنَ سَمَّاهُمْ رَسُوْلُ اللهِ ﷺ وَبَشَّرَهُمْ بِالْجَنَّةِ ، نَشْهَدُ لَهُمْ بالجَنَّةِ ، عَلَى مَا شَهِدَ لَهُمْ رَسُولُ اللهِ ﷺ ، وَقَوْلُهُ الْحَقُّ ، وَهُمْ: أَبُوْ بَكْرٍ وَعُمَرُ وَعُثْمَانُ وَعَلِيٌّ وَطَلْحَةُ وَالزُّبَيْرُ وَسَعْدٌ وَسَعِيْدٌ وَعَبْدُ الرَّحْمَنِ بْنُ عَوْفٍ وأَبُو عُبَيْدَةَ بْنُ الْجَرَّاحِ ، وَهُوَ أَمِيْنُ هَذِهِ الأُمَّةِ ، رَضِيَ اللهُ عَنْهُمْ أَجْمَعِيْنَ .

٩٦ ـ وَمَنْ أَحْسَنَ الْقَوْلَ فِي أَصْحَابِ رَسُوْلِ اللهِ ﷺ ، وأَزْوَاجِهِ الطَّاهِرَاتِ مِنْ كُلِّ دَنَسٍ ، وَذُرِّيَّاتِهِ الْمُقَدَّسِيْنَ مِنْ كُلِّ رِجْسٍ ، فَقَدْ بَرِىءَ مِنَ النِّفَاقِ .

٩٧ ـ وَعُلَمَاءُ السَّلَفِ مِنَ السَّابِقِيْنَ ، وَمَنْ بَعْدَهُم مِنَ التَّابِعِيْنَ ـ أَهْلُ الْخَبَرِ وَالأَثَرِ ، وأَهْلُ الْفِقْهِ وَالنَّظَرِ ـ لاَ يُذْكَرُوْنَ إِلاَّ بِالْجَمِيْلِ ، وَمَنْ ذَكَرَهُمْ بِسُوْءٍ فَهُوَ عَلَى غَيْرِ السَّبِيْلِ .

٩٨ ـ وَلَا نُفَضِّلُ أَحَداً مِنَ الأَوْلِيَاءِ عَلَى أَحَدٍ مِنَ الأَنْبِيَاءِ عَلَيْهِمُ السَّلامُ وَنَقُوْلُ: نَبِيٌّ وَاحِدٌ أَفْضَلُ مِنْ جَمِيْعِ الأَولِيَاءِ.

٩٩ ـ وَنُؤْمِنُ بِمَا جَاءَ مِنْ كَرَامَاتِهِمْ، وَصَحَّ عَنِ الثِّقَاتِ مِنْ رِوَايَاتِهِمْ.

١٠٠ ـ وَنُؤْمِنُ بِأَشْرَاطِ السَّاعَةِ: مِنْ خُرُوْجِ الدَّجَّالِ، وَنُـزُوْلِ عِيْسَى بنِ مَرْيَمَ عَلَيْهِ السَّلامُ مِنَ السَّمَاءِ، وَنُؤْمِنُ بِطُلُوْعِ الشَّمْسِ مِنْ مَغْرِبِهَا وَخُرُوْجِ دَابَّةِ الأَرْضِ مِنْ مَوْضِعِهَا.

١٠١ ـ وَلَا نُصَدِّقُ كَاهِناً وَلَا عَرَّافاً، وَلَا مَنْ يَدَّعِيْ شَيْئاً يُخَالِفُ الْكِتَابَ والسُّنَّةَ وَإِجْمَاعَ الأُمَّةِ.

١٠٢ ـ وَنَرَى الْجَمَاعَةَ حَقًّا وَصَوَاباً، وَالْفُرْقَةَ زَيْغاً وَعَذَاباً.

١٠٣ ـ وَدِيْنُ اللهِ فِي الأَرْضِ وَالسَّمَاءِ وَاحِدٌ، وَهُوَ دِيْنُ الإِسْلَامِ، قَالَ اللهُ تَعَالَى: ﴿ إِنَّ ٱلدِّينَ عِندَ ٱللَّهِ ٱلْإِسْلَٰمُ ﴾ [آل عمران: ١٩]، وقال تعالى: ﴿وَمَن يَبْتَغِ غَيْرَ ٱلْإِسْلَٰمِ دِينًا فَلَن يُقْبَلَ مِنْهُ ﴾ [آل عمران: ٨٥]. وقال: ﴿ وَرَضِيتُ لَكُمُ ٱلْإِسْلَٰمَ دِينًا﴾ [المائدة: ٣].

١٠٤ ـ وَهُـوَ بَيْـنَ الْغُلُـوِّ وَالتَّقْصِيْـرِ، وَبَيْـنَ التَّشْبِيْـهِ

وَالتَّعْطِيلِ ، وَبَيْنَ الْجَبْرِ وَالْقَدْرِ ، وَبَيْنَ الأَمْنِ وَالإِيَاسِ .

١٠٥ ـ فَهَذَا دِيْنُنَا وَاعْتِقَادُنَا ظَاهِراً وَبَاطِناً ، وَنَحْنُ نَبْرَأُ إلَى اللهِ مِنْ كُلِّ مَنْ خَالَفَ الَّذِي ذَكَرْنَاهُ وَبَيَّنَّاهُ .

وَنَسْأَلُ اللهَ تَعَالَى أَنْ يُثَبِّتَنَا عَلَى الإِيْمَانِ ، وَيَخْتِمَ لَنَا بِهِ ، وَيَعْصِمَنَا مِنَ الأَهْوَاءِ الْمُخْتَلِفَةِ ، وَالآرَاءِ الْمُتَفَرِّقَةِ ، وَالْمَذَاهِبِ الرَّدِيَّةِ ، مِثْلَ الْمُشَبِّهَةِ وَالْمُعْتَزِلَةِ وَالْجَهْمِيَّةِ وَالْجَبْرِيَّةِ وَالْقَدَرِيَّةِ وَغَيْرِهِمْ ، مِنَ الَّذِيْنَ خَالَفُوا السُّنَّةَ وَالْجَمَاعَةَ وَحَالَفُوْا الضَّلاَلَةَ ، وَنَحْنُ مِنْهُمْ بُرَآءُ ، وَهُمْ عِنْدَنَا ضُلَّالٌ وأَرْدِيَاءُ .

وَبِاللهِ الْعِصْمَةُ وَالتَّوْفِيْقُ .

* * *